THE LITTLE BOOK
OF UNSUSPECTED
SUBVERSION

MERIDIAN

Crossing Aesthetics

Werner Hamacher

& David E. Wellbery

Editors

Translated by
Rosmarie Waldrop

*Stanford
University
Press*

———

*Stanford
California
1996*

THE LITTLE BOOK
OF UNSUSPECTED
SUBVERSION

Edmond Jabès

'The Little Book of Unsuspected Subversion'
was originally published in French as
'Le petit livre de la subversion hors de soupçon'

© Éditions Gallimard, 1982.

Assistance for this translation
was provided by the
French Ministry of Culture.

Stanford University Press
Stanford, California
© 1996 by the Board of Trustees of the
Leland Stanford Junior University

Printed and bound by CPI Group (UK) Ltd,
Croydon, CR0 4YY

CIP data appear at the end of the book

Stanford University Press publications
are distributed exclusively by
Stanford University Press within
the United States, Canada, Mexico,
and Central America;
they are distributed
exclusively by Cambridge University
Press throughout the rest of
the world.

Contents

Subversion is the very movement of writing: the very movement of death.

The written page is no mirror. To write means to confront an unknown face.

Driven mad, the sea, unable to die in a single wave.

Blank, like a name left blank.

~

"What is subversion?"
"Perhaps, in the rose that you adore, the least
obtrusive thorn."

The book thrusts its rhythm on the body, the
mind.
Free rein, then, for subversion.

Whatever you do, it is yourself you hope to
save. It is yourself you lose.

Truth knows all shades of subversions.

"If our place is what detains us, mine will in the end have been a fetter, a humiliating hobble," he said.

For place, all you will have had is the hope of a mild place beyond the sands: a mirage of repose.

Life adds. Death subtracts.

> (All creation takes for its place an enclosed space surrounded by the infinite.
> I shall have torn down walls everywhere, offering to my books, beyond their own space, an infinite, forbidden space.)

There is a time for allegiance. March time or mark time. Subversion always demands our immediate, full commitment.

Subversion never relents. You stop it by making it shift targets.

Like the dark at the foot of night, subversion can issue only onto itself.

To live means to adopt the subversion of the moment; to die, the irreversible subversion of eternity.

"The cadence of subversion. Ah, I had to find again this cadence," he said.

You have not created. In your small sphere of action, God-like, you create but for the moment.
Subversion is a pact with the future.

"At its peak subversion is so natural, so innocent, that I might be tempted to consider it one of the privileged moments when our precarious balance is restored," he also said.

Menace is illegible.

~

If the word enlightens, silence does not obscure: it regenerates.

Banality is not harmless: blue shark.

("Banality is no stranger to subversion. An ally of time, which discounts it, it is subversion banalized," he said.)

Subversion hates disorder. It is itself righteous order as opposed to reactionary order.

Knowledge knocks against the cold scope of ignorance, like sunbeams on the mirroring sea, dumbfounded by its depth.

(There are no exceptional actions. There are only natural actions, but among them some major, some mediocre.

There is creation.)

Sages and madmen of my books, you who have made me familiar with subversion, your place is here. Nowhere. In the sand where I have often lain, without yet wanting to die, and let my hands open to the void.

Subversive prophets of the arid kingdom where I have joined you, you have filled my years with your phrases, riddled my sky with insistent questioning, buried my certainties under your feet.

"The universe is a book; every day, a page of it. You read a page of light—of waking—and a page of dark—of sleep—a word of dawn and a word of forgetting," he had noted.

The desert has no book.

A raging sea hounds the sky with its bounding
questions.

It is an exhausted ocean, sunk back into the passivity of water that you can bathe in.

> Shadows without shadow,
> lights without light:
> clear traces of oblivion,
> and, here, the mystery of the road.

God is God's Silence remaining silent.

The Prince's slave and the courtier's have the same
status of slave.

To descend into yourself means discovering subversion.

The Question
of Subversion

("We threaten what threatens us. Subversion is never oneway," he had noted.

Through its title and the work that already contained it, this little book hooks onto the ten volumes of the Book of Questions. *This also is no doubt subversive.*

If I give the same title to two different texts, arbitrarily imposing on them a unity of circumstance, do I not oppose them all the more to each other?
The conflict is internal.

Thus the word that names us is the same that, sooner or later, violates the ineffable Name of God; for no creature can bear the absence of the divine name.

Had he not written: "Through His Name, God is at the mercy of man?"

The revolt of a shadow hastens the coming of light, just as the illegible, at war with itself, prepares us for the perfect reading.

We need continuity, resemblance, reciprocity, as we need fresh bread.

Man is both his own origin and his own beyond.

It takes only a smile to stop a tear. It takes only a tear forever to shatter a smile.

"The subversive does not necessarily proclaim itself as such from the start. On the contrary, in order to act more surely on the beings and things it defies, it often sides with them unreservedly, to the point of speaking in their name.

"In this way white can topple white into a fatal abyss of whiteness by claiming to be whiteness itself," he said.

Nothingness remains the unconscious stake of subversion.)

"I have only bad disciples," said a sage. "Trying to copy me they betray me; believing they resemble me they discredit themselves."

"I am luckier than you," replied another sage. "Having spent my life questioning, I, of course, have no disciples at all."

And he added: "Is this not why I was sentenced for subversive activities by the Council of Elders?"

"A knot cannot make another knot, but any thread can.

"Hence every knot is unique.

"It is the same with our relation to God, to mankind, to the world," he said.

Thought has no ties: it lives by encounter and dies of solitude.

"Look at me," he said, "listen. I am the perpetual questioning that refills the well.

"It is the well you see and hear. In the hour of thirst you bend down to drink."

To every book its twenty-six letters, to every letter, its thousands of books.

Trembling, he handed his teacher a notebook filled with handwritten words: his book.

"Why are you trembling?" asked the teacher.

"These pages," he answered, "burn my fingers like sheets of ice. I'm trembling with cold."

"Tell me what is in these pages," the teacher continued.

"I do not know," he replied.

"If you do not know who will?" said the teacher.

"The book knows."

> (*A blind man* locks up *looking, as a dumb man, speech. Both are repositories of the invisible, the unsayable;*
> . . . *infirm keepers of Nothing.*)

"What follows is to be followed. It is no tributary of what was, but of what will be," he said.

~

These pages bear witness to how impossible it is to come to terms not only with our thought, but also with ourselves. They tell our discomfort in facing how markedly inept we are at being.

All duration is tied to memory.

After reality comes an unreality more than real, which our memory appropriates.

Thinking follows an opposite path. It approaches absence and, unfolding, helps plot its course.

Thought is a lightning bolt rending the void. Oblivion, its

momentary space. Our dim memory of it would, then, work at recouping thought by means of a new space, would zealously instigate a confrontation of thought with both its past and its probable development, would take responsibility for putting it in tutelage for good.

On one side freedom; on the other, fetters.

A prisoner of thought, could God be subject to the universe? The unthought—His inconceivable nonduration—would then, alone, perpetuate Him in secret, for eternity is also limpid nonduration escaping perceived duration.

God is a stranger to time as to duration, since He is without extension.

> *("Are absence and presence two pieces of glass
> meant to fuse?
> "In that case, the punty is thought," he said.)*

"We have nowhere sufficiently stressed," he had noted, "that thought, having come out of a previous thought—not necessarily the most recent—will either lean on the continued influence of the latter or act in distrust of it.

"This would let us suppose that thought has a recall of its own, and we do not know if it is totally dependent on ours or not.

"O complexity of memories, which we tell one by one, lacking experience of their entanglements and final scope."

No memory is innocent.

Oblivion is the stillborn memory within all memory, which afflicts recall.

"*To precede*," he had added, "must also be taken in the sense of *to forestall.*

"The thought that precedes a thought has sometimes forestalled it in breaking new ground, forcing the second thought to cede it place.

"This is why we can never say precisely which of the two has been thought first.

"We have good reason to believe that thought's own memory recalls both its triumph and its inability, at any given moment of its history, to be; recalls moments of pride and humiliation that remain unperceived by us."

Every thought has its joys and its bruises.

Thought pays attention only to the reactions of thought.

"You think: you imagine, reflect, and dream all at once.

"No sooner is it mastered than your thinking sends you back to your imagination, your reflections, and your dreams.

"You will never have the upper hand," he said.

"You will always be on the bottom, in regard not to what you think, but to what you still need to think," he also said.

"You think in order to know. You do not even know your thought," he had written.

"Day is tied to consciousness. The unconscious is opaque night.
"See how paradoxical, the whims of God.
"On the one hand, He appeals to consciousness to develop in us the idea, the sentiment, of the divine; on the other hand, by prohibiting the image, He throws us back into the unconscious, where He reigns without us," he had noted elsewhere.

Nothingness, our eternal place of exile, the exile of Place.

The stone, indifferent to God and man in its hard solitude, we shall let watch over nothingness.

~

Images founder in the unconscious, but do not fade: glimmers of oblivion.

He said: "Images in the unconscious are like underwater fauna and flora. The diver's quick torch tracks them down.
"Once out of the water they are but ill-assorted objects, an undeciphered alphabet of dead memory, often the cause of inner lacerations."

We live by recouping mournful images, whose number we can never guess.

The oldest, without question, is that of God, which God Himself does not remember.

Image of the first day.

Image of death denied us until death.

Legibility posthumous.

Little Limits to
the Limitless

... fecundity of death, O word, its would-be
radiant point of birth!

I

For God, God is nothing other than Himself.

No matter what the distance, it is always thinkable: small, it is prey to our eyes; immeasurable, prey to the imagination.

"The longest line comes out of the shortest, which is itself the point's unappeased desire to go beyond," he had noted.

"The infinite does not give us the measure of All or Nothing, fulfillment or void, but of the incomplete," he said.

"In vain the line promises the infinite a desired end," he said.

"What if God needed a shadow to cast doubt on Himself?
"This shadow could be the book, which is perplexity of light and the distress of night," he said.

And added: "Heirs of the Book, all the fortune at our disposal is the bit of obscurity and of light handed down to us. Ah, all our words are but a work of shadow, figures of our consuming lack."

"If a shadow is a question for the light, it is also a question for the shadow; if light is the shadow's answer, it is also light's. O wheel within wheel," he said.

"The shadow is not lack, but fullness of void where the stars are shining. Black, black of Nothingness," he said elsewhere.

The dimmest glimmer, and we surmise a universe.

"What are your eyes?"
"Those of my book."
"What are your ears?"

"Those of my book."
"What is your breath?"
"That of my book."
"What is your hope?"
"That of my book."
"What are your chances?"
"Those of my book."
"What will be your death?"
"What lies in wait for me on the last page of the book: death of all our shared deaths."

If God were *One* He would be double, since the unique is only the unthought form of the *One*, which, no sooner thought, stops being unique.

No step will ever be resigned to being only a step, *one solitary step.*

II

> *("Any book unable to resist events is no book," he had said.*
>
> *"Time has always gotten the better of events," people had retorted.*
>
> *"Then the book is time," he had concluded, "a time without the strength of time, but with all the weakness of eternity.")*

The work is never done. It leaves us to die unfulfilled. It is this empty area we must not so much occupy as tolerate. Here we must settle.

To accept emptiness, nothingness, blankness. All our creating lies behind us.

Today I am—once again—in this blank space, without voice, without gesture, without words.

What remains to be done is always only what would claim that it is done: the desert where we are buried by our impotence.

To tell oneself that the end—the sought-after limit—is impossible. A consolation, surely, for most of us. Distress for those lost under the spell of the unknown.

Limits transgressed within their limits: our daily bread.

The extremes will always remain unknown to us.

~

You write with lowered eyes—but eyes that hold the sky.

There is only one sky, just as there is only one page.

Our vocables: constellations in the night of thought; in the morning of the unthought they are invisible.

Shadowless pages of the Book of God, dazzled pages of man's book.

We can question only Power. Nonpower is the question itself.

The question is made of darkness. The answer; brief light.

The answer has no memory. Only the question recalls.

("*It could be that fulfillment is only a comforting form of the unfulfilled: the only one visible,*" *he said.*

"*... all in all, a chance for unfulfillment to become aware just how unfulfilled it is,*" *he added.*)

The Page as a Place
to Subvert Both Whiteness
and the Word

Subversive, the page where words believe they will find a foothold; subversive, the word where the page opens onto its whiteness.

One step in the snow is enough to shake the mountain.

The snow does not know the sand. Yet the desert is in both.

Glacial, whiteness at its peak.
Black, the sun of the word.

The marriage of paper and print—of white and black—is a coupling of two subversions fighting each other at the very heart of their union, and at the writer's expense.

Apparent harmony most often masks an internal brawl. The eye sees only what comes into view.

In the most obvious things, subversion finds its ideal field of operation.

You write. You are ignorant of all the conflicts your pen raises in passing, where the book is at stake.

The truly subversive book is perhaps the one that denounces both the word subverting the page and the page subverting the word by fusing them in the wake of assailed thought.
To make a book would then mean to support the respective takeovers of these subversive forces, which run through language as through silence.

Subversion is the favorite weapon of both the unusual and the everyday.

"Our relation to God," he said, "is an indirect relation to subversion."

Any word said aloud is subversive in relation to the words kept silent. Sometimes subversion works through choice, through an arbitrary choice that is perhaps a necessity still obscure.

Subversive Himself, how could God have thought that man would not be so toward Him?
God created man in the image of His subversiveness.

And if subversion were only the gap between things created and things written?

One and the same abyss would then separate man from man and book from book.

("Divine or human," he said, "the 'I' is the theater of all subversion."

"The art of living," he also said, "the high art of subversion! Here is perhaps the beginning of wisdom.")

Outside Time,
The Dream of the Book

You think you are dreaming the book. You are
its dream.

What is a dream but the erased writing of a
book that writes itself in this erasure, and that
we read with closed eyes: the lack—lacuna,
omission, deficiency—of a book?

Writing would mean granting the dream image the abstract reality of the sign.

There is no dream but in forgetting a word.

The road to my book is a road opened up by ten paths.
Do you remember?
Sand has long swallowed them.

All that is left are undatable ridges shifting with the wind;
for the book never stops venturing outside the book.
Following its trail means wandering forever.

"Even the most solid fortress is subject to the slightest
sagging of the ground," he said.

"There is no path we cannot point a finger at, but what hand
could lay hold of it?"
"None, for sure. Any, however, could destroy it."
What to conclude from this if not that nothing, not even
God, is spared death; for thought, eyes, and hand work for it
alone.

"Death does not kill. We kill, every single moment, for
death," he said.

"Burned by ancient absence, a lively, subterranean light is
kindled in the desert by one grain of sand rubbing against
another. O common desire for eternity! O mute spark of love
in my sore heart," he wrote.

"Of the passion of book for book only vestiges remain.
"Our days and nights were but the ardor and torpor of this
mad sentiment," he said.

"Any book is the docile object of the contradictory desires it
inspires in the book that writes it," he also said.

~

"Open up God: an abyss," he said.

To turn your name into a rosary of unassigned names.

Ed, who had it from Emo, who had it from Nod, who had it from Don, who had it from Seb, who had it from Jassé, who in turn had it from Bes, who had it straight from Sébaya's mouth, said: "There are no books but in the death of the Book. Its own death writes them. But this writing is doomed never to find a grave."

And he added: "For a valid definition of the book I would gladly sacrifice all the works in the world. For it is through this lack of definition that our books have so far been able to force themselves on us as enigmas to be deciphered."

"Close the book," he said, "and to the cosmic shadow you add the burden of a shadow in confinement."

"The writer's despair is not that he cannot write a book, but that he must forever pursue a book he is not writing.

"Of this pain I have spoken only once. O that your brotherly word could now take over from mine," he also said.

~

"God is both saved and undone by the book. So the glory and misery of the word teaches."

"God needs the caution of His Word; and the Word, the caution of the Book."

"God provides reading matter. He does not read."

"Writing a book consists perhaps in giving the deciphered moment, through the expedient of each of its words, back to eternity."

"It is not only a word you form in writing it, you also delimit a moment of your life," he had noted.

("We speak to break our solitude; we write to prolong it," he said.)

Of Solitude as
the Space of Writing

> "Dawn," he said, "is but a gigantic auto-da-fé of books, a grandiose spectacle of supreme knowledge dethroned.
> "Virgin then, the morning."

The gesture of writing is a solitary gesture.

Is writing the expression of this solitude?

Can there be writing without solitude or even solitude without writing?

Could there be degrees of solitude—hence several planes, different levels of solitude—as there are gradations of dark or light?

Could we, then, maintain that certain solitudes are pledged to the night, others, to the day?

Could it be, in fact, that there are various forms of solitude: a round, resplendent solitude—of the sun—or a flat, somber solitude—of gravestones? A solitude of feasts and a solitude of grief?

Solitude cannot be uttered without immediately ceasing to be. It can only be written at a distance, protected from the eye that will read it.

Then *utterance* would be to a text what the spoken word is to the written: the end of a solitude taken on by the former and the prelude to solitary adventures for the latter.

Whoever talks aloud is not alone.

Whoever writes rejoins, through the mediating word, his solitude.

Who would dare use speech in the middle of the sands? The desert responds only to the scream, the ultimate, already swathed in the silence that gives rise to the sign. For we always write at the blurred confines of being.

To become aware of these limits means, at the same time, to recognize writing's point of departure: the irregular demarcation of our solitude.

So both solitude and writing have fluctuating boundaries, which we skirt, pen in hand. Boundaries honored by us and thanks to us.

To each book its lair of solitude.

Seven heavens claim the sky. Emptiness has levels. Likewise solitude, which is the emptiness of heaven and earth, the emptiness of man, in whom it stirs and breathes.

Tied to all beginnings, solitude has the exceptional power to break up time, to isolate the original unity, to turn the indeterminable *multiplicity* into an innumerable *one*.

Under these conditions, trying to write would consist in retracing—though backward—in the margin of the written, the path thought had followed; in leading thought back to the very object of its thinking, and the written to the vocable that already contained it. It would, in short, mean coming out of our own solitude in order to take upon us the initial solitude of the book still ignorant of its beginning, which the book will name. For it is on the ruins of a book we have abandoned that a book is built, on the frightful solitude of its rubble.

The writer never leaves the book. He grows and breaks down by its side. It could be that the first stage of writing is simply gathering stones from the collapsed book in order to cement them into a new work—the same, no doubt: an edifice for which the writer is untiring foreman, architect, and mason all in one; less attentive, however, to the progress of construction than to the natural inner movement that presides over its completion; attentive, above all, to writing this double solitude—of the word and the book—that would gradually become readable.

Nowhere but in this thin paper rectangle reserved for the unsayable are words and their dwelling place so strongly tied together and at the same time—O paradox—so distant; for solitude is granted no alliance, no union or association, no hope of common liberation.

Alone, it erects itself. Alone, with the complicity of writing, it arranges to read the proud walls from the times of its splendor or of its wide, deep wounds, in an hour when the work it helped put on its feet falls to dust, when the book breaks apart in the infinite breaking of its words.

Solitude that the writer submits to, to which he sometimes grants more than he can keep, unable to withdraw from the commitment he has made.

But why? Is solitude not a deliberate choice of man? So what are these chains he has not forged? Could there be a solitude that escapes his will, that he, powerless, can only suffer?

The demands of this solitude, from which the writer cannot come free, have been laid on him precisely by the word that designates it; solitude from the rock bottom of solitude, as if

there were a solitude yet more alone, buried in solitude where
the word models itself on its own captive image like a child in
his mother's womb.

Hereafter everything develops in premeditated order, for the
project of the book is first of all the daring project of the
vocable. We cannot write a book without indirectly participat-
ing in this daring, which is perhaps our intuition of the book,
from which the book will grow.

Solitude of a word, then, solitude of the word before the
word, of the night before night, immersed in which a star, the
vocable, shines for itself alone.

But, you will object, how can one get from the book to the
word? As day turns toward the sun, I would reply. Is "book"
not a word? It is always to the *word* "Book" that we return. The
book's space is the inner dimension of the word that names it.
So writing a book means occupying this hidden space, means
writing within this word.

As the morning star gathers all the light in the world, this
word gathers all the words of the language and yet is but their
place of solitude; the place where it faces the void, where it
ceases to mean and no longer designates anything.

"You cannot read your life, but you can live your reading,"
he said.

~

"How many pages are in your book?"

"Exactly ninety-six level surfaces of solitude. One under the
other. The first on top, the last at the bottom. Such is the
advance of writing," he had replied.

And had added: "What intrigues me is not how, sheet after sheet, I went down all the steps of the book, but how, to begin with, I managed to find myself on the highest, the first."

The bottom of the water is strewn with stars.

~

Writing is a wager of solitude, flux and reflux of anxiety. It is also the reflection of a reality reflected in its new origin, whose image we shape deep in our jumble of desires and doubts.

The Ante-Dwellings

"Before the house, question the threshold.
The stone is already counterbalanced there," he
said.

Everything was in the wait for God.
Thus Creation preceded the Creator.

. . . God coming thus before God in the Idea
of God.

Everything was in the wait for Nothing, and
Nothing preceded our wait.

God *is* for having answered the question: "*Are you?*"

"If the existence of God came after that of man, nothing
would keep us from thinking that the void had a voice older

than that of the world, and that the desert, so close to emptiness, spoke before the dawn that shook the dark.

"Stifled voice of the sea. Drowned voice of sand," he said.

The question creates. The answer kills.

God died of His premature answer, to which man bowed
down.

God speaks from the farthest point of death. From the
beginning, we have listened for this silence.

Is the book our ante-limit?

In that case we write only for death. Writing, once arrived at
the point where there is no more writing, would abandon us to
the void.

"The difference between our books and the divine Book is
perhaps this: the former must traverse life to reach God, the
latter only death to come to us," he said.

The double of One is one.

The interdict on images saves the double.

Book upon book! The sacred Book spreads its transparency
over the forbidden book.

One does not proceed from the sacred to the profane, but
rather from the profane to the sacred.

As one proceeds from a silence peopled with words to a silence returned to its initial absence.

~

Exclusive, the consonants safeguard the illegibility of the divine Name: house walled shut.

Vowels are the melodious song of morning.

"Our soul is a nest of vowels. A bird stands at the beginning of the infinite reading of the world," he also said.

What comes before dwellings is perhaps a potential word.

("A word can never be a dwelling," he said, "yet it too has its foundation and its passages."

An utterance is an inland valley with a passion for sea breezes. O unquenched desires! O invincible voyages!)

The interdict defends the horizon.

The Interdiction
on Representation

"Why," he was asked, "is your book just a
sequence of fragments?"

"Because the interdict does not smite a book
that is broken," he replied.

But had he not recently jotted in his journal:
"I write a book to give back to God the entire
image I have made of Him with words.

"Would writing, under these conditions, not
mean perishing of the divine wrath?

". . . to perish of a forbidden image at the
heart of all images?"

"We cannot read erasures," he said, "but we can imagine
reading what has been erased for good.

"A reading of death."

"We only read what is lacking from the total reading of the word," he also said.

"So that, each time, we are led to read it differently."

Who could further a reading of the interdiction which any reading of the book tries to revoke?

Only one who has already led a word from silence to silence.

Out of this infinite distance that separates absence from itself he could then, up to the inevitable surrender, risk such reading.

"You exhibit what should not be revealed. In fact, you merely give a glimpse of what your intended object hides behind.

"And this *behind which* may very well be another object.

"Spiteful interdict," he had written.

"God is full of spite, for if we cannot see His Face it is because, of all the faces we scrutinize, His is the one that cannot be shown or contemplated, which allows any face to find in its acquired independence the freedom to deceive, namely, to be at the same instant appreciated both for itself and as the fortuitous, fleeting projection of an unknown face," he had also written.

God escapes the lie through a more eloquent lie, which, quick to denounce any other, ends up forcing itself on the believer as his only truth.

~

What if the divine interdiction struck, first of all, Truth?

The real image of God would yield to the constant pressure of an absolute absence of image which relentlessly seeks it out, to annihilate it.

The object delights in its absence. Likewise, the Creator in man, and the creature in God. To the point where each is but the absence of a reclaimed absence, the temporal nature of this absence in the offered face, which is itself only the desired—rewarded—abdication of the first and last face.

Truth would be the dramatic end of any story that has God as its hero and man as an extra.

And if the divine interdiction struck at the very Idea of God?

Double and identical sacrifice. The original story would be deciphered on the surface of the sea that swallowed it, at the spot marked by its disappearance.

We can read only ripples left by a shipwrecked word and gradually smoothed out by the calmed waters.

Then only the careful wave would be left to enforce the interdict.

~

"The interdict lies within the dictum, not like the stone within a fruit, but like the sun within the night it sets on fire," he said.

Of any unsupported thought the interdiction makes an unthought without rival.

"If light is forbidden to the dark because lethal, what is this undefinable brightness I perceive above us?"

"Perhaps a knife whose fine blade gleams in the night and which God uses to separate night from day, like halves of a single fruit."

~

All writing is a fertile field mowed, in season, by death.

This is why the scythe of time is the interdiction's best weapon.

"There is a time for *making* and a time for *mowing*: one and the same time," he had noted.

~

"Are true books just books? Are they not also, like the words of Sages, embers dormant under the ashes, according to Rabbi Eliezer?"

—Emmanuel Levinas

"Do you know," he asked, "how grains of
sand in the desert sometimes get that greyish
hue? It is not the approach of night, but the veil
of ashes that covers our futureless books."

If you want your words to be words of God, you must make
your interim book a book of eternity.

But if we believe Dov Baer from Mezeitz, who wrote, "The
Saint, blessed be his name, dwells in every letter," your book
has been eternal even before being written.

It is through its divine aspect that a book survives time.
What to deduce, unless that this divine aspect is within us as a
foreboding of a time reserved from eternity?

The Word of God has been silent since the day when, in
order to be heard, He enjoined silence on our human words,
forgetting that it was through them that He spoke to us.

The silence of the Word of God is but the infinite silence of
our crushed, common words.

We cannot attain the silence of God except by making it our
own. Recognizing the Word of God would then mean accepting our own silence.

To say this silence means to say the sacred, but also, at the
same time, to undo it.

There is no one sacred Book, but there are books open to the silence of the sacred Book.

To write on the basis of this silence means to insert the Book of Eternity into the mortal book of our metamorphoses.

~

("*Thou shalt not make a book in the image of the Book, for I am the only Book.*

"*Nor shalt thou make the ragged, fearful word into a word of glory;*

"*for thou canst write only what thou art, and I have wanted thee dust.*"

Thus God might have expressed Himself; but does He not often proceed by allusions?

"*Do not trust what is said clearly, because clarity is only the more welcoming slope of darkness, and the Word of God keeps clear of either side,*" *he had noted.*

Could there be a sun for the dark? It would not be a star, but a blazing secret.)

~

"What is a sacred book? What confers on it the character of the sacred?"

"Does the sacred depend on us?"

"Would a book of knowledge be a sacred book? No, because knowledge is human."

"We say: 'In this book there is the word of God. Therefore it is a sacred book.' But is it not we ourselves who, trying to reveal, formulate this word?

"Could the Word of God be this silent Word that breaks its silence in each word of ours?"

"Then there would be no sacred book, any more than a profane book: there would be the book.

"But which book? The absolute Book of God, the incomplete book of man?"

"The book is both presentation—it presents, presents itself—and representation—it reproduces, tries to stabilize.

"But has God not forbidden any representation of Him?"

~

What if the divine interdiction of representation were also found in writing, as both its implacable law and its share in the curse?

What if the sacred, being the Word of God, were only the silence of our words?

What if the profane, being emancipated speech, were but a challenge to divine silence?

Then image would be to word as absence of image is to silence.

Profane and sacred would find themselves swept into an inevitable showdown.

To write under the constant eye of God would mean a tireless effort to reproduce nothing but His Word; yet reproducing this Word, do we not in spite of ourselves introduce images into the text?

~

"Are true books just books? Are they not also, like the words of Sages, embers dormant under the ashes?"

Still, we must specify what books are meant here. What is a true book? Could there be false books?

The true books, if they are books, are also "embers under the ashes." Could this *also* mean that their fate is to be consumed while consuming others to the point of being nothing but the force of this consummation? As if consuming other books, far from defeating them, gave them, on the contrary, a renewed, unfailing vigor?

Are the true books, then, those that continue to die of the death of the others?

But perhaps the embers reddening under the ashes are only the sage's Words, surviving the book?

The true books, in that case, would be those that have stopped being books in order to be only the Word of the sacrificed book, word of this sacrifice, in mourning for a book.

. . . in mourning for a book that, after all, is nothing but mourning for a place. But this place is also God in one of His innumerable names.

What is the future of this Word without place?

In other terms, could there be a future for the sacred, without its exemplary Word being annexed by place?

If there is no place for the sacred except in an abyssal absence of place, then what is a sacred book? It would have to be on the scale of this Word, would even have to be this Word, both outside time and anchored in a time vainly striving to consume it while consuming itself, which, with this act, would impose on it the status of an audible, readable Word.

Then there would be, on the one hand, a free, sovereign, sacred Word and, on the other, an indefinite space man would try to circumscribe, which is perhaps the book: profane book, tributary of our vocables, but raised by their closeness to the sacred Word to the latter's level.

Then the book would be the boldest human enterprise: with the goal of providing a place for a unique, universal Word—the sacred is indivisible—and permitting the vocables gathered around it to surpass themselves in death.

The book, in this hypothesis, would come before the Word, which, being at first silent, would come before the book that reveals it. Word of silence, maintaining this silence at the heart of any word, but also Word approached, intercepted in the bedrock of this silence, which, in a mysterious return to beginnings, is the virginity of the book.

So there are two books in one. The book within the book—sacred, austere, ungraspable Book—and the book that opens to our curiosity; profane work, but transparent, in places, to the presence of the Book hidden in it: the sudden limpidity of an inspired word, so airy, so dazzled, so avid to last that it hurls us for a brief moment into the heart of an adumbrated, white, naked eternity. Eternity of the divine word, of which the word saddled with man is a desperate echo.

"A people of priests" obedient to Yahweh's commandments, the Jews recognize themselves in one Word only: the sacred, holy Word. The profane word does not have the freedom of the city.

In Hebrew, sacred and holy are one and the same word, but can we really say that the sacred is the holy and vice versa?

One and the same word, true; but like a cracked nut the left half of whose shell would, for example, hold the sacred, and the right half, the holy, and whose kernel would have the primary savor of silence.

So the sacred would not be the holy so much as a sacralized inner silence heavy with all silences; and the holy, not so much the sacred as the holiness of the gift.

Could it be that God puts profane words in man's mouth? And man, sacred words in the mouth of God?

Having been the trenchant, definitive answer, the sacred is mute. It comes before and after the question.

Writing, interrogative even in its affirmations—and always in question—is our weakness and hence the domain of the profane.

Since saying, bound to the moment, means utterance abolishing all utterance, absolute writing—considered as writing of the sacred—could only be the silence of speech.

Writing outside time, always *beyond*, yet readable in the words it transcends: a writing out of bounds then, outlandish even, which would weigh on our writing with the infinite weight of absence and would make it face its limits in its own dependence on an unlimited of which it is the poor expression.

. . . in its dependence, then, on the silence it would vainly try to pierce, not in order to reduce it, but to survive.

The path from a book to the absolute, silent Book—an immutable word can only be silent—is the path from personalized words to impersonal Word; just as the path from the absolute Book to a book is that from the Word of fire to words in flames.

But who can draw the dividing line?

In the beginning was the All, and All was the sacred word, and the sacred word was infinite silence undisturbed by any noise, any sound, any breath.

Once man had conceived of it, All was engulfed in Nothing, and Nothing was vocabulary, and vocabulary was the book, and the book was mischief.

Will we ever know the extent of this mischief?

The act of writing defies all distance. Is it not every writer's ambition to raise the fleeting—the profane—to the level of the lasting, the sacred?

Thus writing, from one work to the next, would be the effort of words to exhaust saying—the moment—and take refuge in the unsayable, which is not what cannot be said, but what has been so intimately, so *totally* said that it no longer says anything but this intimacy, this unsayable totality.

Then profane and sacred would be only prelude and finale of one and the same commitment, which, for the writer, means to live his writing all the way to the threshold of silence, where it will abandon him; unbearable silence from which a surprised universe emerges only to get lost, in turn, in the word that takes it on.

If one admits that in principle it is the profane that troubles, disturbs, feverishly challenges, one might deduce that the sacred in its disdainful persistence is, on the one hand, what freezes us in ourselves, a kind of death of the soul, and, on the other hand, the disappointing outcome of language, the last petrified word.

So it is in relation to, and through, the profane that we can experience the sacred, not as sacred, but as the sacralization of the profane's passion for going beyond, as infinite prolongation of the minute rather than as an eternity alien to the moment;

for death is the business of time.

Is it not precisely through the word, unable to appropriate saying, that eternity becomes conscious of being incompatible with language?

An invisible God needed an unpronounceable Name.

Writing—being written—would then mean passing, unaware, from the visible—image, face, a representation lasting the moment of an approach—to the invisible, to nonrepresentation stoically combatted by the object; from the audible, which lasts the space of a listening, to silence, into which our docile words plunge to drown; from sovereign thought to the sovereignty of the unthought, remorse and supreme torment of the word.

The sacred remains the unperceived, the hidden, the protected, the ineffaceable. Hence writing is also a suicidal attempt to take on the word, even to its ultimate effacement, where it stops being a word and is only the trace—the wound— of a fatal and common divorce: between God and man, between man and the Creation.

Divine passivity, irreducible silence in the face of the unforeseeable and perilous adventure of the word left to itself.

Coming before the profane, this is the arbitrary excess that constantly pushes back any boundary.

Sacred. Secret.

Could it be that the sacred is the same as the eternal secret of life and death?

There is a day after, a night after, which day and night must invariably confront.

They are promise of dawn and certainty of coming dusk. Here, life and death, profane and sacred, touch and intermingle, like sky and earth convinced that they form one single universe.

The original interdiction gives nonrepresentation its sacred character. The language of God is a language of absence. The infinite admits no barrier, no wall.

We write against this interdiction, but is that not, alas, to run the more violently afoul of it? Saying is never more than a challenge to the unsayable, thought no more than a denunciation of the unthought.

At the heart of the book, the face prohibited deals a mortal blow to the human word in its likeness to the divine Word.

So the sacred book must be read through God's rejection of man's book, refusal that initiates its destruction. Writing in the wake or shadow of the absolute Book would, at this stage, mean accepting this refusal.

The Book of God remains the undeciphered Book, whose cipher is the live red among ashes of doomed truth, which it behooves us to feed forever.

At this close range, writing would consist in rewarding with secret words a book destined to dissolve in the margins, a book whose provisional illegibility would, through its lack, allow infinite readings of our works.

There is a bit of sky within every patch of land, and ink shines sometimes with a light more intense than a dazzling break of day.

God created man in His image, which He erased by erasing Himself.

Man, not having known the face of God will, a fortiori, never know his own. He knows only the pain of loss. He knows that what passes for his face is, after all, only the longing for an absent face.

Could it be that God's image is that of an infinite erasure? In this case man's image would also be, and their resemblance, that of an absent image to an absence of images; a resemblance, finally, of Nothing to Nothing.

Trying in spite of everything to have a face means that the creature, in his stubborn will to exist, had to invent it.

But all creation is bound to a fraction of time, which, deprived of a future, is itself an erasure.

Then what is the face we show? Could it be simply the image of an image we claim as our birthright?

Behind it there is no doubt the true face emerging from its erasure and forever being erased in its new traits: face of sand, sculpted in sand.

We can only question it, starting from the void.

The book closes always on a lost face.

The Three Jacket Texts of
the 'Book of Resemblances,'
Restored to the Sand

The life and death of sand are but one and the same approach of day and night, freed of time, for which the desert is cradle and final bed.

It is on resemblance that sand lives, of its speckled emptiness that it dies.

The resemblance of one grain of sand to another is perhaps that between shards of a mirror at the moment of shattering and those of a mirror broken centuries ago.

There is no resemblance save at the price of abdication.

∼

The Book of
Resemblances

Do we read a book through its resemblance to a lost book? Is every book a book of resemblances? Is resemblance the unmasked place of the book? Are we only our resemblance, a thousand times baffled, to ourselves?

A book is to be read. It "resembles a book that was itself not a book, but the image of an attempt."

We encounter "characters who resemble characters we have known, but who were themselves only heroes of fiction."

A new *Book of Questions*, presented as both its own arbitrary double and tyrannical opposite, sees the light. This light makes us tackle a reality till now hidden behind its precarious appearance and, in turn, reopens a totally committed questioning.

(1976)

~

Intimations   The Desert

Could the difficulty of being hinge on the name? As if it could be translated only by a name we cannot bear?

Does the questioning of the name I have pursued from volume to volume since the first *Book of Questions*—followed by *The Book of Resemblances*—does this implacable questioning not in fact call ourselves into question through the word that carries and rejects us?

Does any allegiance we fully pledge originate—O mockery!—in our ascertaining that it is impossible to belong, a knowledge so unbearable that we allow ourselves to deny it so as not to perish?

But the book is perhaps only one stage on the road toward the horizon, where everything gets simpler. For only death is simple.

At the heart of our *intimations*, exacerbated by each of its words, at the threshold of the *desert* where it leaves us, the book, named by what it names, can only be the infinite opening and closing of the name.

(1978)

~

The Ineffaceable   The Unperceived

It might be that all books are contained in the last from which they were drawn. Book before all books. Book of unlikeness, which the others try to resemble. Intimate model unmatched by any copy. Mythical book. Unique.

With this book, the writer would know both the immense joy of having at last expressed himself completely and a panic fear of having nothing more to say, when, on the contrary, the completion of this book would finally give him back his words. But what would he do with them?

Have I reached the end of my doubts and fears, my hopes and my anxiety?

Have I, in this hour of closing the book forever, reached my own end?

What picture of the universe could I subscribe to at this

point? None in particular, or—who knows?—the one sug-
gested by the book: picture of a sun that no longer warms the
earth, but burns the sky.

It brings home how excessive our solitude.

(1980)

~

*("The frontiers of language are our own borders.
"On this side, there is the thought of man. Is
there, on the other, the unrevealable Thought of
God?" he had written.*

*"We might in a pinch understand the acts of
God, but never the confounding Thought that
rules them," he had also written.)*

Of Thought as Creation
and Destruction of Being
Through the Word

To lose a night is to harvest a thought.

"Thinking pulls back the thick veil covering
the universe, only to replace it with another so
thin we barely guess it is there.
"We perceive the world only through this
transparent veil," he said.
And added: "What if this veil were language?"

I think. Am I my thoughts?
In order to think my thoughts I must myself be thought.
—Thought only speaks to thought, as word only to word.
If I am my thought, I am also its rigging and hence the
movement of the Void that carries it and carries it off: Void on
which we build, in the heart of which we founder.
Am I the Void of my thought? In that case thinking would
not mean "being" but *permitting* thought to blaze its trails.

But how could I permit, without already existing? And what are these trails unless already mine?

Remains to be known if *I* think, and therefore *am*, or if *I am* because thought thinks in my name; I being no more than the frenzy of my thought's advent, no more than the glimpse gained of my body—that dismembered site where thought sounds.

I sustain you with my words; the same words retain us.

"God says 'I.' How could man, after Him, say 'I' when speaking of himself?"

"Perhaps because 'I' is but the void filled by one and the other. By one through the other."

Purity of silence! Not of the silence that knows, that has listened and repeated, but of the silence that has forgotten.

If the unthought is a blank, how could we help surmising that perhaps behind it a thought timidly prepares to be born?

Thought forms by intertwining what is thought—its boiling past—and what is unthought, its problematic future: a plain knot or one with a brand name.

The future too has its morning after.

"The unthought is daily surpassed; which reinforces, if possible, my conviction *that there is no pause for thought.*

"Like death, which comes before and after life, the unthought would then be the uncheckable measure of thinking, which is constantly tested by its failure," he wrote.

And added: "There are those who claim we cannot go beyond the unthinkable precisely because it strips us of all thought. I would reply that, for a thinker with a passion for pushing beyond, the unthought resides in the image of a threadbare void revealed by a cut knot that a new knot is about to replace."

And he concluded: "The life of thought is a sequence of sorry knots sacrificed to its permanence."

Had he not written: "What has been thought and what remains to be thought are the same thread, its strands twisted together by the unthought. We tighten our knots around an absence of thought that acknowledges the degree of their strength."

Inexplicable, our behavior before a rose.

In love with its beauty, with an admiring gesture, we take its life.

Writing means applying this gesture to ourselves.

What dies in us can only die with us.

The book is the daily announcement of all such deaths.

Of the Key Word as
Creation and Destruction of
Being Through Thought

"We are quick," he said, "to confuse obsessive words with key words.

"A key word is not necessarily an obsessive one. Often, on the contrary, it is an unnoticed, unsuspected word.

"In order to open a door one must put the key in the lock. What does the owner of the key do afterward? He puts it in his pocket.

"We are not going to ask him to show it to us. Its barrel, pipe, teeth do not excite our curiosity.

"Every key is made to open a lock and then disappear from sight.

"We are never obsessed with a key unless it is lost.

"In a piece of writing, the key word plays the same role. It is the word that opens the text to the text, hence to us.

"It is not the beginning word, but the word where everything begins. It may be found at the beginning as often as at the end of a page of writing, or as in the middle, or as just after the first words or before the last.

"One can never be sure to recognize it because it generally operates in secret. But its gesture is luminous.

"In vain do we try to pin it down. It is the word that all the words of the text, falling into place, pronounce—but so softly that it cannot be heard by anybody: *mysterious password*, behind which stands the book."

"And what if the key word were not a word, but a key any word could use? This would mean we cannot enter a book except in collusion with the word that holds the key to the door we happened upon: key word of circumstance.

"Writing would then only facilitate this trading of keys among words. This is what I shall call the instinctive relation to the text," he also said.

"It is obvious," he had noted, "that the word 'azure' evokes the word 'sky,' but does not reveal it. The word 'void,' on the contrary, could.

"If I write, 'Before it was black, the void of my soul was blue,' I cover with this one phrase the whole reach of the sky."

"It is not the writer," he had also noted, "who holds the key to the text, no more than the text as it opens to be read. It is what the words have not been able to imprison.

"The key no doubt is this lack, betrayed in the book by various words that themselves carry an immemorial absence: lack within an infinite lack.

"What we don't see is what allows us to see."

All silences are joined in the three letters of the first and last silent word: God.

Three is the number of the infinite.

God's key ring is buried in the Text. This divine gift to the vocables is at the root of their intimate and mad ambition.

All thought depends on the caprice of a key.

The space of a word could not be closed off by either man or word: it is imaginary.

Imagination has its limits: an outrageous reality.

To imagine means to create more. This "more" cannot be specified.

Imagination is perhaps only a thought that has cast off the ballast of its origins; the daring of a visionary word at the sudden edge of the universe.

Even the smallest pebble is suffused with the infinite.

Absence as Origin,
or, the Patience of
the Last Question

The first question is asked by the last.

Patience of marble. The tree is its constant care.

"I have gathered for you thirty-two similar pebbles.

"Sixteen are questions of life; sixteen, questions of death.

"Mix them, for each of these vain questions can only be answered by an equally vain question," he had written.

And had added: "For each question a stone, for the thousands of graves I lie in."

To learn to be patient without, for all that, turning your back on impatience.

To oppose a secular patience to the impatience of the question.

To be the target of all questions—target that provokes questions.

To take on the endurance of the target.

To multiply the question by whetting its impatience and, at the same time, cultivating the patience that allows it to persevere.

To hound the answer. To turn the hounding against yourself.

To be the one who wounds and the one wounded.

It is in death that truth blazes with all its light.

The event prevails.

"The event," he said, "is one of the perforations in the left margin of my pages, perforations that one day will let me tear them off without damage, so I can give them intact to the wind: my final gift."

And he added: "Eternity is dotted with abysses: our everlasting everyday."

You think you live, you think you write your life: you dig a hole.

The everyday is running water, duration its filter.

What has happened was foreseeable. Nobody tried to avoid it.

Without weakening, night waits for the sun.

Only what touches us closely preoccupies us. We prepare in solitude to face it.

He said: "Indifference is a venom we sip like chilled fruit juice in summer."

Horror predominates. Pain folds in on itself.

Circle of murderers. The ringleader is not always the one we suspect, even on good grounds.

"We do not judge the victim, but the murderer. The victim has already been judged: judgment by murder.

"How many of you subscribe to this? How many of you deny it?" he had written.

~

He said: "A child's face, not yet molded by language, is a face outside time.

"The time of a face is the time of its wrinkles."

He also said: "The first face is a tender appeal to all the faces it prefigures; the last, the sum of all our withered faces."

Identity is not so much apprehending a face as winning it over.
An alliance with death.

Any thought of death involves destroying the face. We cannot think identity outside nothingness.

God wastes man in God.
Cruelty of Nothingness.

Nothingness can only be thought by reducing all thoughts to nothing.

There is no absence that time does not already consider its well-deserved recreation, its legitimate rest, its seventh day.
Reality, marked by time, thus joins for a brief moment the eternity of an unreality that has imagined it and to which it in turn has unwittingly given existence.
It is to this time, cut off from time, that absence belongs.

Absence is to presence what all is to nothing: one and the same stupor.
. . . what dreaming of a dream is to reverie.

~

"I was spared time," he had noted. "I would have been my own dream."

He said, "I have no place," as you might say, "I have no ties," knowing all the time that every word creates its place.

There are moments that are born and die in a moment. They will never be accounted for.

Of what remains, I am the lesser misfortune: a burnt straw.

The question at the heart of the everyday is both the moment in question and the question of the moment.

Eternity is without questions.

The answer should respond to the interrogations of the moment, as it should to the interrogations of the question itself; but, stubborn, it only responds to itself.

Eternity is back of time.

Between the void and the unthought lies the whole course of thought: from its nocturnal unfolding to its curtailed end.

To believe you still have something to say even when you no
longer have anything to express.
Words keep us alive.

We die always of a frustrated word.

The moment is rich with glimpses of, and encounters
with, eternity, as the hoisted sail is drunk with space and
spindrift.

Insensible eternity!
The sky disappears into sky, and the sea into sea, without
causing the least disturbance or inspiring compassion.
The loss of the moment has short- or long-term conse-
quences only for what buds and what breaks down.

For the sky, the ocean, night means neither grief nor sleep,
but an impasse.
The sun plays eternity against the moment.

Sizing up the moment means, perhaps, flouting eternity.
Out of a handful of sand scooped up in the desert you do not
separate one grain in order to weigh it.

Light above our dim lights. Dazzled thought.

Blind, the seer's thought.

("You cannot write on sand; it would mean writing over your own words, over a text already disclaimed by the sand," he said.)

"I am hostage of a word that is, in turn, a hostage of silence," he said.

"Death is first of all in the word.
"So do not look for mine amid the feverish throng, but where they fold back on their late eternity," he said.

We do not think death, the void, emptiness, Nothingness, but their innumerable metaphors: one way of getting around the unthought.

My books have been written, not in or with sand, but by and for the sands.

Books whose fate—an immobile adventure—I took on by deciphering them, all the while identifying with them to the point of being nothing but their writing. A miracle made possible at the price of my own undoing.

Sands that in the name of Nothingness abolish Nothingness, could I evict you from your lawful share in the infinite?

The sky wins out over the book, but not over the sands that congeal it in every grain.

Only the weight of silence can be thought here.

God did not carve His word into stone, but into the eternal moment of petrified silence.

The breaking of the Tablets is the fundamental act that allowed divine writing to pass from silence into the ratified silence of all writing.

Riches of supreme poverty.

"Writing," he said, "is an act of silence directed against silence, the first positive act of death against death."

("Beyond what I might still have to say.
"Your portion to read. Mine, to disappear.
"Intruder," he had noted.

"It is the sky that descends onto the earth, not the
earth that rises up into the sky. Our planet does
not, alas, have the lightness of blue, of darkness," he
said.
*   And added: "Thus death will descend on our*
stiffened bodies.")

The written is binding. Perhaps we write only to *disengage*
ourselves without realizing that this is a manner of respecting
our engagement to the last,
    . . . to the last, that is, to the point where, come to its end,
the engagement we have honored appears to us in the form of a
new one.

∼

We read—as we cut grass—what the night will take from
us.

Thought must stoop to conquer new heights. Its peaks are
also its limits.
    This is why we might say the unthought is thought that
cannot be made to stoop.

We are the prey of various scriptures.

"If truth existed," he said, "it would be our only enemy.
"Luckily it does not exist, so we are free to invent our enemies."

"I have studded the night with demands," he also said.
"Some have wanted to take them just for stars in love with their glitter."

All time inheres in a glance.
The infinite opens our eyes, the instant closes them.
No eternity but in oblivion.

He said: "Generous and merciless word. You granted or denied me everything, including the moment that today swells my heart with love and the one that will soon make it beat so feebly only watchful death will hear it."

Any reading sets limits. An unlimited text is one that every time gives rise to a new reading while partly escaping it.
What still remains to be read is its one chance of survival.

To live without asking "Why?" means dodging in advance the question "How to die?," means accepting a death without origin.

The history of thought is perhaps only the daring thought of history lived close to the level of thought—like a branch cropped back to the trunk.

An endless book can find completion only in that of its unforeseeable prolongations.

The air you breathe makes you restore it to the air.
Such is the nature of breath.
Your chest is too narrow for the heavenly gift.

"I am no doubt the memory of my books. But to what point have my books been my memory?" he asked.

Thought is not born to the light. It is light.
Would I, for my part, say it is born to the night?

"I love," he also said, "those fleeting thoughts caught between the haze of sleep and the first timid glimmers of day;
"between the already less dark nothingness where they lay submerged and the flowering grass surprised by the first look."

How is thought defined? Not by what it is, but by what it homes in on.
Then what we call thought is perhaps only its capacity to encircle what is offered.

So we never know how far its curiosity will take us, while it, to match our faith in language, also subordinates thinking to the unforeseeable success of its formulation.

Thought: a ciliated, winged, tufted grain.

He compared thought now to a wheat field, now to an ocean. He was twice wrong. Thought bears the charge of a grain and the dimensions of an ocean.

Bastard thought, poor fountain.

Thought running to seed. The unthought has no stem.

~

"The unthought," he said, "is the beyond of the book, its inner horizon."

If I try to define the unthought by comparing it to a certain ferment, it immediately seems, rather, the infinite torment of my thinking.
So what is beyond the book is still the book.

I cannot think the unthought except by starting from the limit.
The region I head for is uncharted.

Any step belongs to thought.
To the unthought: the sudden lack of rungs.

To know every interval of the infinite, like the layout of a house.
The moment is a minuscule door into duration. We enter, once again small.

In my house, time finds no shelter.

"I can say without risk of error," he had noted, "that the unthought is nothing but the feared crumbling of a bridge between two hazy shores."

The earth turns in the bold thought of its roundness and in the unthought void that supports it.

What has the power to undo cannot be undone.

We always write along the thread of Nothingness.

To say of thought, as of a fruit, that it has set.

No way out but into the unknown.

The man who leaves—Abram—where does he go? Sets out in search of his identity and discovers the *other*. He knows from the start that he will perish of this *otherness*, in the unfathomable distance separating him from himself, out of which rises the face of his solitude.

We live on this side. We die, always, on the other; but the line is in the mind.

Can we think otherness? We can only draw on our idea of it.

Could our relation to the other be but the relation of two barren thoughts set heel to heel, where the unthought does not yet dare flaunt its triumph?

Likewise day and night at bay, faced with perishing by their own weapons.

Aging wounds us. All our setbacks are bloody. But sometimes, at the lowest point of the curve, a spark of love is enough to brighten our night.

Never consider an acquisition as anything but a manifestation of Nothing's irony.

Having possessions means, in a certain way, living on the salutary humor of emptiness.

"The thinker is a seasoned fisherman," he said. "From the sea of the unthought he draws luminous thoughts—moonfish, globefish, pilotfish, flatfish—which, having swallowed the bait, wriggle for a moment between the blue of the sky and the blue of the sea before they stiffen, aliens, on the ground."

Terrifying couple: life atremble, death in stitches.

Thought is to life as the unthought to death: one and the same buoy.

For living as for dying, we will have used the same bobbin.

As a bedlamp lights only the space between bed and wall, freedom illumines but the shadow of one step.

It seems absurd, at first sight, to ask questions of absence. Yet all our questions are really addressed to it.

"We rush so blindly toward the vast realms of absence that I am frightened.
"All becoming is but absence gradually assimilated," he said.
And added: "My soul has had its best part amputated, as a healthy body may lose its right arm.
"Ah, how its hurts me, physically, this missing part of myself.
"What can I conclude if not that absence is revealed in pain?"

Blood reddens the ink without, for all that, warming it.
Every word dies of exposure.

Our absence from the world is perhaps nothing but our presence in the void.

You can only count the days you lose.

A glance whose solitude we could never imagine: the glance of the Void.

Hide your wounds from the man who bears you ill will: they would excite him.

"What is frightening you?"
"What settles down in your name and needs no justification."
"I do not follow."
"And what if I told you your truth is murderous?"

~

(If God is His Word, the desert is older than God, being the place where it first appeared, hence older than His Word. But God is without past. Do we admit, when we say God is born of God and dies in God, that He is at the same time Word and Place?

By declaring, "I am the Place," did God want to

point out that He was the Word of all places and
the Place of all words?
    God's life was disconcertingly brief; His death,
that of His Word blasted.
    Of this life the desert bears witness in its silence.
Every grain of sand refers us to this death.)

Having opposed God to God, Thought to Thought, Book
to Book, you will have destroyed one by the other;
    but God survives God, Thought outlives Thought, and the
Book the Book.
    It is in their survival that you will continue to provoke them.
    The desert is followed by the desert, as death follows death.

(There is no wounding but is wounded.)

M E R I D I A N

Crossing Aesthetics

David E. Wellbery, *The Specular Moment: Goethe's Early Lyric and the Beginnings of Romanticism*

Edmond Jabès, *The Little Book of Unsuspected Subversion*

Hans-Jost Frey, *Studies in Poetic Discourse: Mallarmé, Baudelaire, Rimbaud, Hölderlin*

Pierre Bourdieu, *The Rules of Art: Genesis and Structure of the Literary Field*

Nicolas Abraham, *Rhythms: On the Work, Translation, and Psychoanalysis*

Jacques Derrida, *On the Name*

David Wills, *Prosthesis*

Maurice Blanchot, *The Work of Fire*

Jacques Derrida, *Points . . . : Interviews, 1974–1994*

J. Hillis Miller, *Topographies*

Philippe Lacoue-Labarthe, *Musica Ficta (Figures of Wagner)*

Library of Congress
Cataloging-in-Publication Data

Jabès, Edmond.
[Petit livre de la subversion hors de soupçon.
English] The little book of unsuspected subversion /
Edmond Jabès ; translated by Rosmarie Waldrop.
p.   cm. — (Meridian)
ISBN 0-8047-2683-3 (cloth : alk. paper). —
ISBN 0-8047-2684-1 (pbk. : alk. paper).
I. Waldrop, Rosmarie.   II. Title.   III. Series: Meridian
(Stanford, Calif.)
PQ2619.A112P4813   1996
848'.91407—dc20
95-38273
CIP

It was typeset in Adobe Garamond and Lithos
by Keystone Typesetting, Inc.

Original printing 1996
Last figure below indicates year of this printing:
04 03 02 01 00 99 98 97 96

Printed and bound by CPI Group (UK) Ltd, Croydon, CR0 4YY

19/12/2024

14615163-0002